Christmas Around the World

COPYRIGHT © MCMLXXXI BY MUSEUM OF SCIENCE AND INDUSTRY/CHICAGO
PUBLISHED BY IDEALS PUBLISHING CORPORATION
MILWAUKEE, WISCONSIN 53226
ALL RIGHTS RESERVED. PRINTED AND BOUND IN U.S.A.
PUBLISHED SIMULTANEOUSLY IN CANADA

ISBN 0-8249-4009-1

Introduction

Christmas, the most widely celebrated of holidays, is observed on every continent of the world. Each nation has incorporated its own unique customs and traditions into the Christmas holiday. The story of the birth of Christ has inspired numerous songs, legends and practices, all adding to the general storehouse of Christmas traditions.

From the earliest days of Christianity, festivals have been held to celebrate the birth of Christ. The word Christmas most probably derived from the name given by the English to their festival, **Christes messe**, meaning Christ's mass. Since the exact date of Christ's birth was not known by the early Christians, the dates of Christmas celebrations varied. Some churches commemorated the event in December, and others observed it in January, April, or May.

The pagan winter solstice festival was perhaps most responsible for setting the date of Christmas. The Romans, Gauls, Teutons and Britons worshiped the sun as the giver of life and light. Their celebrations took place at the time of the shortest days of the year, when the sun seemed to stand still for twelve days before beginning its upward climb signaling spring and the renewal of life in the world. The Nordic people thought of the sun as a wheel or **hweol,** and most likely it is from this word that the term Yule is derived.

The Romans celebrated their Saturnalia holiday from December seventeenth to December twenty-fourth. January first was another important holiday, Kalends, which marked the beginning of a new year. These two great holidays were cele-

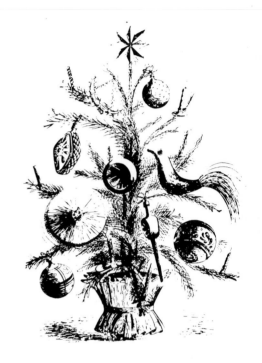

brated with much feasting, merriment, and the exchanging of gifts. Homes were decorated with evergreens, symbols of eternal life; and Yule logs, brought indoors and placed upon the hearth, were believed to burn away misfortune.

Around A.D. 336 the Roman Church finally established the twenty-fifth day of December as the birthday of Christ. Since the fifth century, that date has been celebrated by most of the Christian world.

Today, as in the past, the traditions of Christmas in every land center mainly around the family, hearth and home. Singing the old familiar carols, trimming the Christmas tree, and exchanging presents with family and friends are all part of the many ways Christmas is celebrated around the world.

Regardless of race or geographical location, and within the wide orbit of Christian faiths, the celebrations of Christ's birthday are similar, for the special magic of Christmas is for everyone.

English Christmas tree

Both Christmas and New Year traditions in Armenia are mainly religious in nature. Strict fasting is observed the week before Christmas, ending only after Christmas Eve communion.

That night, the homes are illuminated with candles, and the family enjoys a meal together. The children then gather in groups on the housetops to sing songs of rejoicing. They are rewarded with cookies, candy, fruit, and small coins.

It is also customary for village priests to visit the homes of their congregation and bestow blessings on the members of the household.

At the Christmas Day church service, water is blessed and taken home by members of the congregation to be used for purification throughout the Christmas season. In the homes, it is mixed with earth and kept in a special bowl to be used for symbolical cleansing of dishes and other household objects.

There is much visiting during the next three days of the Christmas season, the third day being especially set aside for the women to visit one another.

Special round, thick cakes with raisins and almonds are made for the New Year's visiting. It is believed that good fortune is granted to the person who finds a hidden coin in his piece of cake.

Armenia

"Schenorhavor Dzenount"

Traditional Armenian dress and Christmas tree decorated with white doves

Christmas in Austria means a whole month of joy and excitement as well as religious fasts and feasts.

It was during the Christmas season in 1818, in the village of Oberndorf, that Franz Gruber gave to the world the music of the beautiful hymn "Silent Night." The story goes that the church organ was unfit for use and the priest, Joseph Mohr, talked over the situation with the organist, Franz Gruber. As Mohr walked through the fields wondering what to do for music for the Christmas service, the words of the lovely hymn came to him. The next morning, he repeated the verses to Gruber who immediately wrote the melody. That night, on Christmas Eve, Mohr sang his song to the accompaniment of Gruber's guitar.

The Advent wreath appears in many homes as the first outward sign of the season. Nearly every Austrian household also displays a Nativity scene, beautifully carved wooden creches that have been passed down in families for generations.

The popular custom is to keep the Christmas tree, which is usually fir or pine, in a locked room until Christmas Eve. After Christmas Eve supper, the Father reads the story of the **Christkind;** then a bell is rung, and the tree is exhibited in its full glory. The Austrian tree is decorated with **Kripps,** which are carved-out fruits filled with tiny scenes of the Nativity.

In Austria, Christmas stollen, crescent cookies and Viennese coffee are enjoyed at holiday time.

Austria

"Froehliche Weinachten"

Silent Night, Holy Night

China

"Kung Ho Hsin Hai"

While Christmas has been celebrated in some sections of China for over four hundred years, the vast majority of its large population has never heard of Christ. The Chinese New Year's celebration is far more common than the observance of Christmas.

Those who do celebrate Christmas, which is called **Sheng Dan Jieh,** or "Holy Birth Festival," enjoy the bright, colorful decorations of the season adopted from their missionary friends. They like the red berries and green leaves of the holly, the bright tinsel and sparkling lights. To these decorations they have added their own attractive Chinese lanterns.

The Chinese Christmas tree is called the "Tree of Light," and its decorations are usually paper chains, flowers and banners on which Chinese characters, meaning peace and joy, are inscribed. To lend an even greater oriental motif, paper models of rickshaws, butterflies and moths are used, in addition to silhouettes of ancient Chinese temples and mobiles resembling Chinese kites.

On Christmas Day, gifts are exchanged, but custom dictates that valuable gifts such as silks and jewels be reserved for the immediate family only. Gifts of food or cut flowers are commonly exchanged with more distant relatives and friends. Children hang up their stockings and welcome toys as their western cousins do. Santa Claus is known as **Lan Khoong** (Nice Old Father) or as **Dun Che Lao Ren** (Christmas Old Man).

Chinese characters of metallic paper adorn Christmas tree

Croatia

"Sretan Bozic"

On December fifth, the Croatian children leave their shoes on their bedroom windowsill for St. Nicholas to fill with candy, fruit and small gifts.

Housewives plant seeds of grain in small bowls of water on December thirteenth (St. Lucy's Day) and place the sprouted plants under the Christmas tree on Christmas Eve. The plants are also placed on dining tables next to a candle and a loaf of bread.

Another quaint ritual, purification by water, is still observed in some sections of Croatia. It is believed that on Christmas Eve, angels pass over the springs of water, touching them with their wings and purifying them. Therefore, the drawing of water on Christmas Day is ceremonious. The water is used in Christmas cake, to bless the house and stables, and a flask is kept in the home to be used throughout the year.

The Christmas tree is decorated on Christmas Eve with handmade ornaments such as painted walnut and acorn shells, heart-shaped designs cut from dough that is baked and painted, and garlands of red and white paper chains.

After midnight mass on Christmas Eve, the family will visit relatives all night long, singing carols from house to house. The traditional **krvaica**, blood sausage, is served, and the celebration includes dancing the **kola** or ring dance to the music of the **tamburitza.**

Mass is again attended on Christmas morning, and a sumptuous feast including roast pork, stuffed cabbage and **orahnijaca,** a sweet bread made with walnuts, is the fare of the day.

Two Croatian girls in national costume

Czechoslovakia

"Vesele Vanoce"

In Czechoslovakia, the Christmas season begins on December sixth and ends on January sixth.

The Czech Christmas tree usually has gaily colored pinwheels that look like snowflakes and twinkling stars. Gilded walnuts and egg shells are decorated as the bodies of strange-looking fish.

Many children still believe that St. Nick descends from a golden cord led by a white-clad angel. The children go to bed early on Christmas Eve, hoping St. Nick will stop at their home and leave a present for them. They often sleep beneath the Christmas table on straw bedding, reminiscent of the humble birth of Christ.

The Christmas menu includes caraway cabbage, roe soup, and Bohemian **kolache.**

In former days and probably in many Czech homes today, party fun was of the homespun variety, and many games and customs were directed at discreet pairing of the young. The young girls had a variety of schemes to get the young men of their fancy in the mood for marriage. For example, little boats were made of walnut shell halves and were floated, holding lighted candles, in a tub of water. The girl whose candle burned the longest could expect to marry in the next year.

Christmas, to the people of Czechoslovakia, means the ending of quarrels and beginning a new year among friends. It is the custom for people to visit each other and forgive any misunderstandings that may have arisen during the year.

Czech girl with dolls underneath gaily decorated Christmas tree

About twenty percent of the Egyptian population is Christian. The Coptic church is the ancient Christian church of Egypt, and Christmas is celebrated on January seventh according to the traditional eastern religious calendar.

Before Christmas, a forty-two day fast is generally observed by the people, and during this time, foods that are derived from animals, such as meat, eggs and milk, are not eaten. Even fried foods are prepared in vegetable oil.

It is the custom to attend Christmas Eve mass around nine o'clock in the evening. The service ends after midnight, and families congregate in a member's home for the early morning celebration. Since the fast ends after midnight mass, much food is available for feasting. Typical dishes that are prepared include various soups and cheeses, roast lamb or other meats, and rice.

Some families exchange gifts and decorate their Christmas trees with the usual bright lights and ornaments. Unique Egyptian trimmings might include camels that are carved out of cypress wood and decorated with brilliant gems, wooden figures of Egyptian musicians, and beaded chains.

Christmas Day is a time for visiting relatives and friends. Liqueur drinks, cakes, cookies, and coffee are served to guests. An especially traditional Christmas sweet is **kahk**, a flat, round cake that is filled with honey and dipped in powdered sugar. **Ghourayeba**, a cookie that is baked with an almond in the center, is also a popular treat.

Egypt

"Id Milad Said"

Wooden camel ornaments, inlaid with gems, hang from Egyptian Christmas tree.

England

"Merry Christmas"

In England on Christmas Eve, the Yule log is traditionally brought inside and placed in the fireplace. According to custom, each person in the family must sit upon the log and salute it before it is lighted, to assure good luck for the house in the new year. Even today a charred stick from the Yule log is placed under the bed in many homes to keep lightning from striking the house.

Religious services predominate the English Christmas celebrations. Processions of carolers gather under lofty arches of great cathedrals at midnight on Christmas Eve to sing cherished hymns and carols.

A typical British Christmas menu includes roast beef, mince pies, plum pudding and trifle, a sponge cake with stewed fruits and custard poured on top.

Wassail, an old Anglo-Saxon toast meaning "what hail" or "to your health," is offered around a large punch bowl. Dating back to 1633, it was often made in the Royal kitchen and known as "lamb's wool." English villagers would take a bowl, usually gold or silver bedecked with ribbons and greens, and fill it with ten gallons of the beverage. It is traditionally made with ale, eggs, roasted apples, blanched almonds, nutmeg, and cloves, and should be sipped while hot.

On December twenty-sixth, the feast of St. Stephen, the English celebrate Boxing Day. In medieval days, the priests emptied the alms boxes of their churches on this day to distribute boxed gifts to the poor, tradespeople, and servants.

Plum pudding—a traditional English Christmas treat

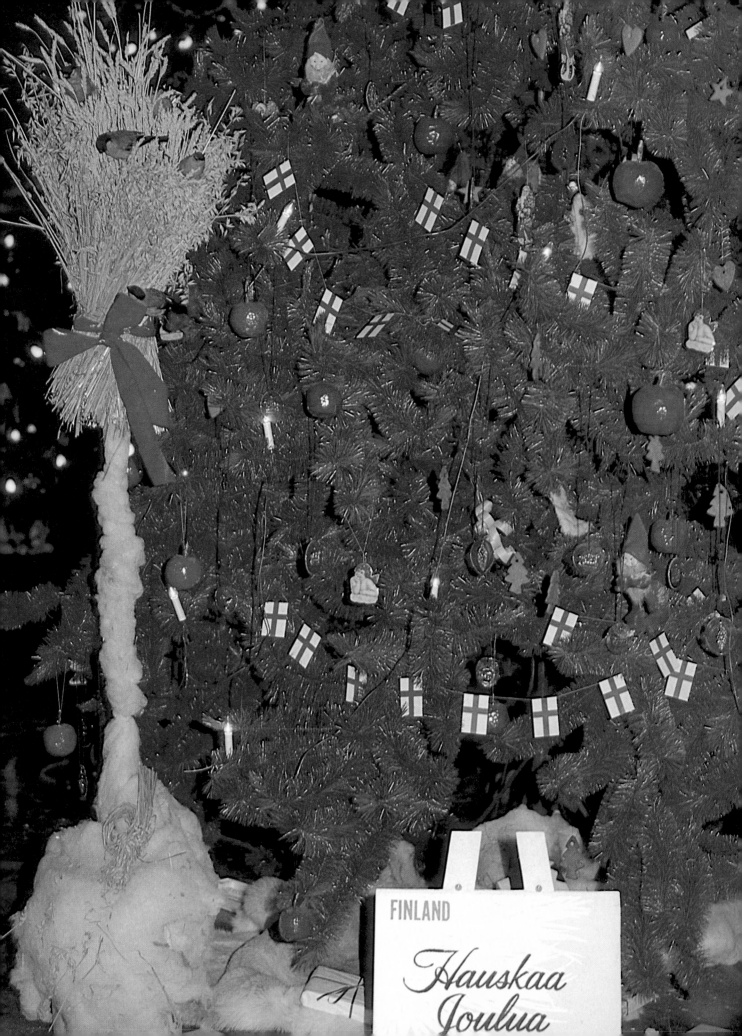

FINLAND

Hauskaa
Joulua

The Finnish Christmas tree is usually decorated on Christmas Eve, displaying scores of candles, paper flags, gilded walnuts, gingerbread cookies, cotton, and tinsel. Sometimes hanging from the center of the dining room ceiling is a **heaven** —a type of Christmas ornament made of brightly colored paper stars, little baubles, silver bells, flags and other ornaments that will reflect the candlelight to make a festive setting for the Christmas banquet.

Before Christmas Eve festivities begin, each member of the family usually takes a cleansing steam bath, and dresses in fresh clothes for the evening meal. Codfish is traditionally served at this meal, along with ham, rice pudding and **torttuja,** a type of plum cake.

Christmas gifts are distributed either before or after dinner. The children are delighted as Santa Claus sometimes makes a personal appearance, accompanied by half a dozen elves wearing red caps. According to legend, the jolly steed that brings Santa Claus to Finland is **Ukko,** a goat made of straw.

Church services are observed early on Christmas morning. Visiting and family reunions fill the rest of the day.

Finland

"Hauskaa Joulua"

Finnish Christmas tree and traditional sheaf of wheat for the feeding of birds on Christmas morning

France

"Joyeux Noel"

In Provence, France, Christmas Eve mass is called the Festival of Shepherds. Shepherds and shepherdesses dress in regional costume and carry a newborn lamb in a procession around the church. A live animal symbolizing the Lamb of God is carried in a wagon, decorated with flowers and lighted candles, drawn by a ram.

The traditional Christmas Eve supper is known as **Reveillon.** Special foods served at this meal include oysters, sausage and wine. In many places this has been replaced by baked ham, roast fowl, salads, fruit, bonbons and the pastries often associated with Christmas Day dinner.

The Yule log tradition was also observed, particularly in the rural areas. The entire family went out to select the tree, which was then cut down. It was carried into the home with much ceremony by the men. The room was circled three times, the log put in the fireplace, and a glass of wine poured over it as the family sang a Christmas song. The disappearance of fireplaces in the city gave a new interpretation to the Yule log. Special cakes, shaped like logs, were baked and then covered with chocolate icing to look like bark, and in this way the edible Yule log became a favorite Christmas delicacy.

French children receive their gifts from Father Christmas. In some areas they leave their shoes on the windowsill to be filled with small tokens and goodies.

The French motif, **fleur-de-lis** (flower lily) is used in decorating the tree, as well as white bonbon ornaments, snowballs and ballerinas.

Intricately constructed creches, with many figures, are commonly seen at Christmastime in Provence, France.

THE SANTONS OF PROVENCE
(A PROVINCE IN THE SOUTH OF FRANCE)

THE ORIGIN OF OUR MANGER OF PROVENCE GOES BACK
TO 1223, WHEN THE FIRST "NATIVITY" WAS STAGED BY ST. FRANCIS
OF ASSISI IN THE FOREST OF THE ABRUZZI. IT COMPRISED ONLY
THE INFANT JESUS, THE ASS, THE OX, AND SOME SHEPHERDS.
DURING THE MIDDLE AGES WERE ADDED THE VIRGIN MARY AND ST.
JOSEPH, THE ANGELS, THE SHEPHERDS, AND THE WISE MEN. ONLY
BY THE END OF THE 18TH CENTURY DID THE FIGURES NOW SEEN
AROUND THE HOLY FAMILY MAKE THEIR APPEARANCE.

THE SANTONS, ALSO CALLED "LITTLE SAINTS", ARE DRESSED
IN THE FASHION OF THE 18TH AND 19TH CENTURIES. THESE LITTLE
STATUES ARE MADE OF RAW CLAY, BAKED IN TWO PARTS, THEN
DRIED AND PAINTED WITH WATER COLORS AND GLUE. ON THE FIRST
OF DECEMBER THOSE LITTLE WITNESSES OF LIFE IN PROVENCE
BRING TO THE INFANT JESUS THE HOMAGE OF THEIR BRIGHT COSTUMES
AND THEIR OFFERINGS. THERE ARE THE ANGEL, THE SHEPHERD AND
HIS LAMBS, THE KNIFE-GRINDER, THE BLIND MAN AND HIS SON, THE
GYPSIES, THE MILL LEADER AND HIS CAMEL, THE PEASANT WOMAN
WITH THE GEESE, THE DRUNKO, THE DIVER, THE HUNTER, THE
BAKER, THE KNIFE-GRINDER, THE MILLER, THE FISHWIFE, THE
CHIMNEY-SWEEPER, THE TAILOR, THE PRIEST, AND AT LAST THE
"INNOCENT ONE", WHO IS PLACED AT THE WINDOW IN THE STABLE.

IN EVERY HOME IN PROVENCE A CRECHE IS INSTALLED AND
EACH DAY THE SANTONS ARE BROUGHT CLOSER TO THE CRECHE. THE
CHILD JESUS IS PLACED IN THE SACRED STRAW IN THE MANGER
ONLY ON CHRISTMAS EVE AT MIDNIGHT, THE 24TH OF DECEMBER.

FUSE

Germany

"Froehliche Weinachten"

A great deal of Christmas tradition is Germanic in origin. When Christianity came to the area of Germany, the word "Yule" evolved from the pagan custom of celebrating the winter solstice, which marked the end of the shortening hours of daylight. The people would light a Yule log in the hearth and believe it burned away misfortune.

In Bavaria today, the Christmas season begins before December sixth with pageants and fairs featuring toys, cookies, breads, gingerbread men, sausages and other goodies for people to buy.

During the remainder of the Christmas season, school children often return to the fair grounds to sing and reenact the Christmas story. The most spectacular of these returns takes place around December twelfth when the children stage the **Lichterzug,** a lantern procession for which they construct their own lanterns in elaborate designs.

Trimming the **tannenbaum** (Christmas tree) is part of the Christmas Eve celebration. Balls of glass, gingerbread cookies, and strips of tinfoil adorn the fir tree, while the top is almost always capped with a star or angel. A tradition-minded German will also light his tree with white candles. Christmas Eve is also a time for singing Christmas hymns and distributing gifts to the children. Later that evening, the family will attend a colorful, candlelight ceremony at church.

A typical German Christmas menu consists of roast goose, spätzle (noodle dough), Bavarian cabbage, pfeffernuesse and Black Forest Cherry Cake.

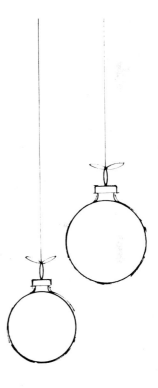

Glittering glass ornaments decorate a German Christmas tree.

Greece

"Kala Christougena"

Bread and water are the principal symbols of Christmas customs in Greece. The bread is a special loaf, baked for the occasion, with a coin placed inside. First, incense is burned, and then, as the family gathers about the table for the evening meal, the bread is broken into small pieces by the parents. The first piece is put aside for St. Basil; the second is intended for the house—that its occupants be blessed spiritually and physically during the coming year. The farm animals receive the third share, and the fourth piece symbolizes material possessions. The remainder of the Christmas loaf is divided among the members of the family. Before it is eaten, each person dips his portion in wine and invokes St. Basil.

Good fortune and prosperity for the coming year are assured to the one who finds the coin in his piece of bread. The coin itself is used to buy a candle to be lighted in church on Christmas Day.

The children of Greece believe they receive their gifts from St. Basil. He supposedly makes his rounds in a boat, which is proper in a country relying on the sea.

After church services on Twelfth Day, or Epiphany, the priests and people gather at a nearby river or spring for the ceremony of "Blessing the Waters." First, a white dove is released over the water as a symbol of the Holy Spirit. The priest then throws a cross into the water and the young men compete to recover it. A special blessing is always given to the one who retrieves the cross, and there is great prestige in being so honored.

The Greek Christmas tree has rows of paper flags and beautiful costumed dolls.

Hawaii

"Mele Kalikimaka"

Before missionaries went to Hawaii, the natives knew nothing about Christmas. Today, however, they celebrate the holiday much as Americans do everywhere.

A most striking feature is the balmy, June-like weather that fills the islands with sunshine and bright tropical flowers. The festive poinsettia blooms naturally in Hawaii, and it is used to decorate homes during the Christmas season.

Fir trees are delivered to the islands by ships from the northwest mainland. It is not surprising that Santa Claus also arrives by boat, and the Hawaiian children marvel at his long voyage from the North Pole.

During the Christmas season, beaches and streets are alive with carolers, singing to the accompaniment of ukuleles. Chinese, Japanese, Hawaiian, Filipino, and Caucasian children join in colorful Nativity pageants. Yuletide **luaus** are also popular, featuring **Kailua** pig as the main course.

The Hawaiian creche is very unique. The baby Jesus, Mary and Joseph are depicted as Hawaiians, costumed in brilliant feathers. The creche is made of bamboo and artificial palm trees with shells and stones as decorations.

On Christmas Day the people will attend church services in the morning and participate in sports, games and merrymaking the rest of the day.

Holland

"Zalig Kerstfeest"

Holland has preserved the bishop's robes of Saint Nicholas, who generally arrives on his white horse on the eve of December sixth, his feast day. In some parts of Holland, he may arrive by boat. The children leave hay and carrots in their wooden shoes for St. Nicholas's horse. A dish of water is often placed there, too. In return, they expect candy and small toys.

In addition to the gifts from St. Nick, Dutch children search the cupboards and cubbyholes of their home in a game of "seek and find." To their delight, a new pair of ice skates or a beautiful doll almost always turns up.

Most families have a tree, usually displaying small candles, and decorate their house with greens and holly.

After church on Christmas morning, townsmen, dressed in grotesque costumes, parade through the streets singing Christmas carols; while the afternoon is usually filled with family activities, a large Christmas dinner, and ice skating on the canals.

Tea and special varieties of hard cookies are served during the "unwrapping" period of gift giving. The table is then loaded with delicacies of the season, small cakes in the form of initials, hot chocolate and roasted chestnuts. Marzipan, the famous Yuletide almond-paste delicacy, is a Dutch favorite.

Overall, the Dutch Christmas is filled with a spirit of friendship and family togetherness.

The Christmas celebration begins in Hungary when the first star appears in the sky on Christmas Eve. Just before the evening meal, the family gathers round the Christmas tree to say a short prayer and distribute the gifts.

The Hungarian Christmas tree is laden with nuts, cookies, and paper cornucopia filled with **Szalon Cukor,** a homemade fudge-like candy.

At the Christmas Eve meal it was customary to set an extra place for the stranger who might knock at the door in search of hospitality. Traditional dishes served included cabbage soup, fish, cakes shaped like horseshoes and filled with poppy seeds or walnuts, special twisted bread, and small dumplings sprinkled with poppy seeds and sugar, called **Bob-ajka.** By custom, crumbs, swept from the floor after supper, were thrown across the threshold at midnight by a girl in search of a husband, and her future spouse's face would appear to her.

At midnight, villagers, dressed in bright costumes, meet at the church to celebrate mass amid a profusion of candles, flowers and evergreens. A beautiful creche is also always on display in the church.

The children will sometimes march through the streets singing Christmas carols and reenact the birth of Christ with marionette figures in a miniature creche.

Hungary

"Boldog Karacsony"

Hungarian girl hanging apple ornament on Christmas tree

Iceland

"Gledileg Jol"

Christmas goblins, or **Jola-Sveninar**, take the place of Santa Claus for children in Iceland. As Christmas draws near, these goblins come down from the mountains to the villages to enjoy the festivities. Children like to believe the little creatures bring their Christmas gifts, and adults enjoy dressing up to represent the goblins.

Icelandic people must either import Christmas trees from Norway or make their own, because few trees of any kind grow in their far northern country. The trees are decorated with homemade wreaths and paper ornaments, and candles of mutton tallow are fastened to the branches.

On Christmas Eve, the family gathers around the tree to sing carols and exchange presents. Lights are kept burning throughout the house, all night long, in honor of the Christ Child, and children are allowed to stay up late.

Icelanders look forward to a special feast on Christmas Day. They enjoy smoked mutton served with **laufabraud,** or fancy fried cakes, **poonukokur** (thin pancakes), and at the end of the meal, a Christmas cake filled with raisins and currants.

The holiday celebrating usually ends on New Year's Eve or on Twelfth Night, when a great bonfire is lighted in the public square. Christmas trees and gift wrappings are thrown on the fire, making a glorious blaze.

Icelandic Christmas trees feature hanging goblins and homemade paper ornaments.

Ireland

"Nodlaig Nait Cugat"

As in England, the Irish love to prepare plum pudding for their holiday festivities; and when friends or relatives stop by on the day it is being prepared, they each take a turn stirring the pudding as a symbol of friendship and neighborliness.

The Irish never adopted the Christmas tree as a national tradition. If they do use a tree, it is generally decorated with shamrock pipes, country hats, leprechaun faces and, underneath, a Nativity scene.

On Christmas Eve, candles are lighted and placed in every window of the house, and doors are left ajar. The candlelight and open door are symbols of welcome and hospitality, assuring the Irish people that a couple seeking shelter for a Baby, who is the Son of God, will not be homeless. The candlelight must shine all night and should only be snuffed out by those having the name of Mary.

Christmas Day is for sharing. Custom dictates that early in the morning, the Irish family must distribute its baked goods, especially a favorite family specialty, the Christmas cake, among friends and relatives.

"Feeding the Wren" is another Irish custom based upon the legend of St. Stephen who, while hiding in a furze bush, was betrayed to his enemies by a wren. On St. Stephen's Day, December twenty-sixth, the young children gather together, obtain a wren, and place it in a cage on top of a furze bush. Then they go from door to door collecting money for charity. In some districts, the children carry the wren with them.

Italy

"Buon Natale"

The Christmas customs of Italy are entirely centered around the birth of the Infant Jesus. St. Francis of Assisi should be credited with much Italian emphasis on the real meaning of Christmas. It was his famous tableau in the little village church of Greccio, in 1223, that originated our modern crib scenes. At first the manger, **praesepio**, was simple and limited to a few figures, but gradually grew to include many visitors to the stable.

Italy never did adopt the Christmas tree to any extent. The Yule log remains a predominant feature in Christmas festivities. Before the log is lighted on Christmas Eve, the children gather around the hearth and are blindfolded. Then each child must recite a sermon to the Christ Child, after which the blindfold is removed, and a small pile of gifts is revealed. In some sections of Italy, the children tap on the Yule log with a wand and ask for the gifts they wish.

For the Italians, Christmas Eve is a family affair when all relatives are invited to a party at which supper is served. Favorite foods include eel, Jerusalem artichoke cooked with egg, and a great variety of sweets of which **cannoli**, a pastry stuffed with cream cheese, and **torrone**, a caramel nut cake are especially favored. After midnight mass, the celebrating continues into the early morning hours.

The young ones also receive gifts on the Feast of the Epiphany, January sixth, when they hang up their stockings in anticipation of the visit of a female Santa Claus, called **Befana.**

Japan

"Shinnen Omedeto"

In areas of Japan where Christian mission work has been influential, Christmas customs are practiced by the people. Sunday School celebrations are similar to those in America, but with an Oriental touch. At these schools Nativity plays are popular, and the dramas are presented in colorful native dress with much pageantry.

Some Christian groups gather together for religious services to pray, sing hymns, and read passages from the Bible. Many Japanese are familiar with popular western Christmas songs, such as "Joy to the World" or "Holy Night," sung in their native language. Sometimes a tea or cake party follows the service, and Japanese cakes are distributed to those in attendance.

Little wind chimes made of glass or mirrors can be found on the Japanese Christmas tree, as well as colored parasols, brilliantly decorated fans, and fortune cookies. Fish ornaments also hang on the tree, since carp is held in high esteem in Japan.

Japanese trees may also display little replicas of Shinto gates, symbolizing the entrances of Shinto temples. In translation, the word **Shinto,** the Japanese state religion, means "The Way of the Sacred."

Favorite treats, especially at Christmastime, are Japanese fortune cookies, made of rice flour and known as **sembei.** They are served with tea and usually contain little slips of paper bearing cheerful messages.

Attractive paper lanterns add an Oriental touch to the Japanese Christmas tree.

Korea

"Sung Tan Chul Chook Wha Ha Myo"

Christmas celebrations in Korea are centered around church organizations and programs. Students in the Christian schools usually present dramas or programs about the Nativity during the Christmas season.

Some homes have Christmas trees decorated with colorful miniature objects easily recognized from everyday life such as Korea's hourglass, drama masks, silk shoes, ladies' purses, and long silk scarves in bright colors. Many families exchange gifts, and the children expect Santa Claus to fill their stockings and bring them presents.

On Christmas Eve, children and young adults gather at church until around two o'clock in the morning when they go out to sections of the parish, singing hymns from door to door. The families wake up and come out to greet the carolers, sometimes asking them to come inside for a small treat.

The people attend Christmas morning services wearing the national costume or dressed in their best clothes. The services contain many beautiful features such as singing by the church choir and the young children, and an address by a special speaker. Along with offerings of money, many people bring packages of rice and clothes to be given to the poor.

After the services, parties are held in the church auditoriums and include sharing tea, cakes, and cookies.

The national dish, **kimchi,** a hot, spicy, pickled cabbage, is usually eaten with the holiday meal.

Top: *Korean girls wearing national costume and Christmas tree decorated with silk streamers and purses*
Bottom: *Tiny costumed figures adorn the Korean tree.*

This country, on the west coast of Africa, received the message of Christianity mainly through mission schools. Children who study at these schools save their **irons,** the native currency, for Christmas offerings and shopping. Items that would be purchased include beads, sugar, peanuts, palm oil and salt.

The Liberian Christmas tree is the beautiful oil palm with its long trunk cut off. It is placed in the dining room and usually decorated with red bells. During the holiday season many homes and buildings are decorated with palms and ferns.

Also at Christmastime, Santa Claus figures dressed in bright costumes, wearing homemade masks, are followed by children as they walk through the streets. The Santas never speak; but when their interpreters communicate the wishes of the children, they dance to the accompaniment of special music played by a member of the group.

Students at mission schools begin singing Christmas carols at dawn on Christmas Day. After prayers and breakfast, gifts are distributed to the children. Many of these gifts are practical, such as cloth for clothes, soap, pencils, tablets, and books. Sometimes there are dolls and a little candy.

Boys and girls from different schools come together for a Christmas program featuring Nativity plays, singing and recitations. Dinner is eaten, as the children sit in a circle on the grass enjoying their special meal of beef, rice, and cookies. Afterward, they participate in games, and the day ends in a blaze of fireworks.

Liberia

"Kwanza"

Lithuania

"Linksmu Kaledu"

Christmas is one of the most important Lithuanian family holidays. For the Christmas Eve dinner, the table is spread with sweet fresh hay (as a reminder of Christ's manger) and covered with a snow-white cloth reserved for the occasion. The meal consists of soup, fish, vegetables, a small hard biscuit served with poppy seed and honey sauce, and an oatmeal pudding. A crucifix and a plate of holy wafers are placed in the center of the table. Dinner begins after the evening star has appeared in the sky. The head of the family begins the meal with a prayer of thanksgiving and a wish that the family remain intact during the ensuing year. He breaks and shares the wafers with each member of the family, who in turn shares with the others.

Christmas Eve is also a time when many superstitions are enacted on the Lithuanian farms. Children will run to the well during the night to see if the water has turned to wine or check on the animals in the barn, hoping to capture the magical moment when they have the power to speak. The hay from under the tablecloth, along with choice bits of food from the evening dinner, will be given to the animals as appreciation for their work during the year and comforting presence in the stable in Bethlehem.

The family will then attend the Shepherd's Mass at midnight or dawn.

Much merrymaking takes place on Christmas Day. Folk singing, dancing and feasting characterize the celebrations. Christmas trees, if used, are decorated with straw ornaments in geometric shapes.

Intricately designed Lithuanian geometric ornaments are fashioned from ordinary drinking straws.

Mexico

"Feliz Navidad"

In Mexico, Christmas festivities begin on December sixteenth, and every home is decorated with flowers, evergreens and colored paper lanterns. A representation of the Nativity, the **pesebre**, is also prepared in each household.

The **posada,** meaning resting place, commemorates the journey of Mary and Joseph and their unsuccessful efforts to find lodging for the night. In some areas, villagers assemble and carry candles, chanting songs, from door to door and return home to kneel at the **pesebre.**

Following the religious customs, a party is held with much singing, dancing and games for the children. One of the features of this party is the traditional **pinata.** This is a large earthenware jar covered with paper to look like a rooster, clown's face, or whatever the maker may fancy. Inside the jar are nuts, fruit and candy. Each child, in turn, is blindfolded, turned around a few times, and then given three chances to break the suspended **pinata** with a stick. Finally, a lucky hit is made, the **pinata** shatters, and pandemonium results as everyone scrambles to pick up the goodies which have showered down.

As in Spain, the Mexican children receive their presents on Epiphany, January sixth.

Decorating the Mexican Christmas tree are red, white and green lights, straw figures, paper flowers, and pottery.

A typical Mexican Christmas menu includes enchiladas, tortillas, large sugar cookies, and Mexican chocolate.

Most Mexican households display a creche at Christmastime.

PHILIPPINES
Maligayang
Pasko

Philippines

"Maligayang Pasko"

Christmas trees are seen in some Filipino homes during the holiday season, as well as decorative flags, palms and colorful flowers.

Urban or rural, mansion or hut, the most basic symbol of the Filipino Christmas is the star of Bethlehem. It hangs in the form of rice-paper lanterns over the windows of Filipino homes in many variations: from common white paper, cut in lace-like patterns, to hexagons and other imaginative shapes. Sizes of these lanterns vary from miniature ones, sometimes seen hanging in automobiles, to giant ones that span forty-five feet.

The traditional modest-sized lantern hung over a window of a house can be easily purchased, but, to many, the custom and spirit expressed by the Christmas lantern requires family creativity.

A star lantern is also displayed in many churches. During the Christmas Eve Mass, at a precise moment, it is released to slide down from the choir loft to the altar.

Colorful wreaths and chains made of brilliant tropical flowers are worn by the Filipino children as they partake in the festive after-mass parade. A band leads the parade, providing music for the children's singing. A family dinner follows the parade. Music, dancing, and Nativity plays provide the days' entertainment.

Concluding the celebrations of Christmas Day, melodious church bells are heard ringing throughout the land.

Two young Filipinos in colorful native dress next to Christmas tree displaying miniature straw hats

The star of Bethlehem sets the theme for Poland's Christmas traditions. The first star in the evening sky on December twenty-fourth signals the end of the Christmas fast and the beginning of the Festival of the Star. In the homes, straw is spread under the table in remembrance of the stable in Bethlehem, and a chair is left vacant for the Holy Child.

Before the meal begins on Christmas Eve, the tradition of the peace wafer is observed. The wafers are small, round and flat, similar to those used in communion. These wafers, previously blessed by the priest, are distributed by the head of the family to all those around the table with an exchange of good wishes. This symbolizes the peace and friendship of those present and comes from the ancient tradition of "breaking bread." The meal follows this simple ceremony, including soup, fish, cabbage, mushrooms, and almonds. Sweets made from honey and poppy seeds are also served. Traditionally, meat is not eaten at this meal. Token gifts such as sugar hearts, cookies or a silver coin are placed at each plate.

It is customary for the young people to go from house to house singing carols, and they are usually welcomed with a glass of wine and cookies.

The Polish tree has a variety of ornaments and will differ in the city and in the country. Red and white, the national colors, are popular in intricate paper decorations.

Poland

"Wesołych Świat"

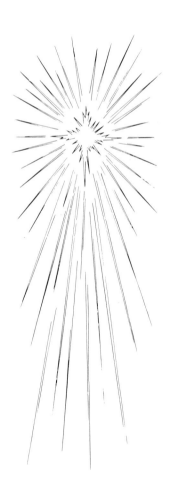

A young Polish girl stands next to a traditional creche that is carried door to door by carolers during the Christmas season. Polish Christmas tree in background

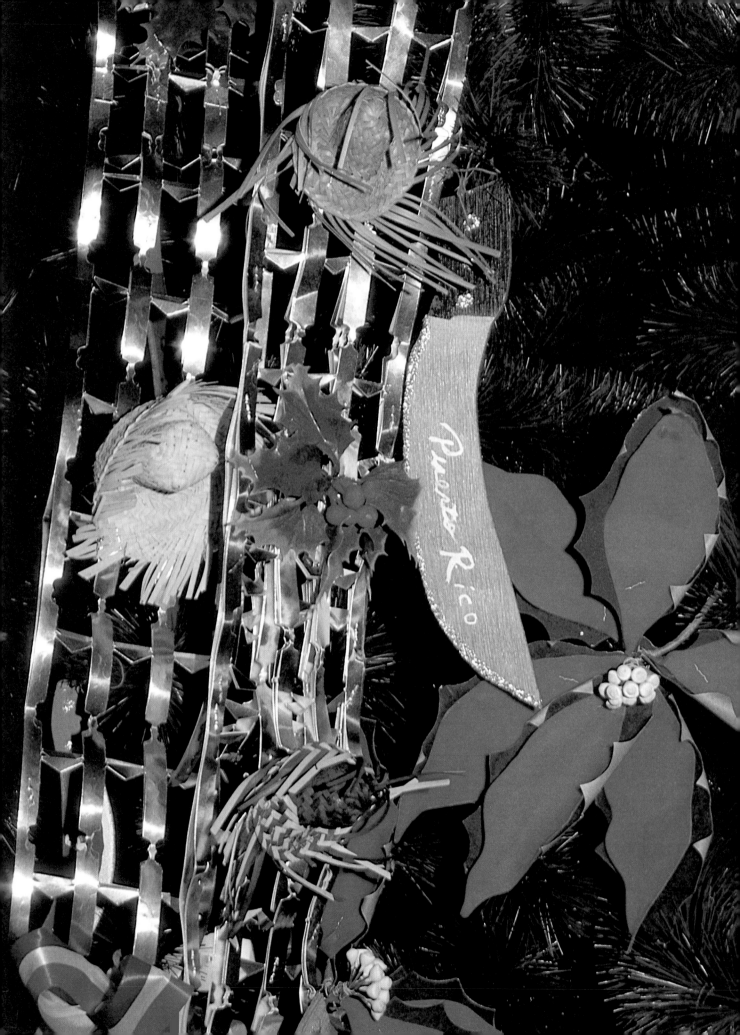

Christmas is celebrated for many days on this beautiful island. The festivities begin on Christmas Eve and continue until Three Kings' Day, the sixth of January.

Homes are lighted and gaily decorated, and the people dress in their best clothes for the Christmas Eve feast. This special feast can be a sumptuous meal featuring a whole roasted pig or a dinner of chicken and rice. Puerto Rican families also enjoy eating **pasteles**—a very complicated tamale filled with ground pork, cubed ham and a variety of other ingredients.

The Christmas Eve feast is a time for families to get together and spend the evening in merriment and singing. Sometimes, groups of musicians go from home to home singing holiday greetings and expecting small gifts in return.

Three Kings' Day is especially exciting for the children, since they believe that the Magi come from the Orient, riding camels, each year at this time. On the night of January fifth, the children fill boxes with grass and place cups of water beside them for the camels. The next morning they run to see the gifts the Wise Men have brought them during the night.

Another happy time for the children is Bethlehem Day, on January twelfth, when they parade through the streets of town dressed in lovely costumes as the Wise Men, angels, shepherds and flute players. The children also carry colorful garlands of flowers in their procession.

Puerto Rico

"Felices Pascuas"

Bright tinfoil streamers and poinsettias decorate the Puerto Rican Christmas tree.

Romania

"Sarbatori Fericite"

In Romania throughout the Christmas season many dramatic presentations of the story of Christ's birth are enacted. Puppet shows are also very popular at this time of year.

From dawn until after sunset on the day before Christmas, boys visit neighboring homes to sing **colinde** or Christmas greetings, for which they receive apples, cakes, and coins.

On Christmas Day they parade through the streets carrying a great wooden star decorated with tiny bells, colored paper, and ribbons. The star is illuminated from within by a candle and is decorated with a picture of the Baby Jesus and the Magi.

Roast pig is the principal food of the Christmas dinner and is served with **colaci,** a wheat loaf. Also served is a symbolic cake called **turte**—layers of thin dough with walnuts and honey, shaped to form leaves, which are representative of the Christ Child's swaddling clothes.

An ancient, but still practiced, Romanian custom is "Blessing the Danube." Clad in gay costumes to depict Pontius Pilate, Herod, and other biblical characters, the people gather at the river bank to sing carols. A young boy breaks the ice, and a wooden cross is thrown into the water. All scramble after it, for the rescuer will have good fortune in the coming year.

The Romanian Christmas tree, displaying a variety of hand-crafted ornaments

ROMANIA

Top left: *Swedish Christmas tree ornaments and children in native dress*
Bottom: *Traditional Norwegian paper ornaments make a colorful tree.*

The customs, like the languages, of the various Scandinavian countries are similar. The days before Christmas are spent in intensive preparation of traditional foods: sausage, cheeses, breads, and cookies for the elaborate smorgasbords. Preceded by herring, spiced fish, and caviar, the meat course is usually goose or roast pig. The traditional drink is **glogg,** a combination of brandy, port wine, and a variety of spices, served with an almond and a raisin in each cup.

One of the most charming customs of Norway is the remembrance of the animals and birds, since they were present at the birth of the Holy Babe. The birds especially are remembered on Christmas morning when every gable, gateway and barn door is decorated with a bundle of grain for their feeding.

Atop the Norwegian Christmas tree, it is customary to place three candles, representing the Three Wise Men. Other decorations include little, elflike creatures, called **Julenissen,** with long white whiskers and red pointed caps.

In Sweden, the Christmas season begins with St. Lucy's Day, December thirteenth, when the eldest girl in each home dresses in white with a red sash and dons an evergreen crown with nine candles. On Christmas morning she wakes the family and brings them coffee and cakes. Many communities choose a Lucia Queen for the pageant and parade held in St. Lucy's honor.

Favorite tree ornaments in Sweden include flags and the **Juldocka,** straw figures in many forms such as boys, girls, chickens and goats.

Scandinavia

Norway—
"Gledelig Jul"

Sweden—
"Glad Jul"

Denmark—
"Glaedelig Jul"

Denmark's Christmas traditions closely resemble those of Sweden and Norway because of their common ancestry. One contribution of Denmark to holiday tradition throughout the world has accomplished an immeasurable amount of good: that is the sale of Christmas seals each year, for tuberculosis prevention.

Scotland

"Nollag Chridheil"

The Scottish do not celebrate Christmas with gay festivities, which they would consider irreverent. Instead, religious services and quiet family gatherings dominate Christmas Day celebrations. Christmas dinner is almost sure to include the traditional Scotch shortbread and new **sowens,** an oatmeal-husk porridge.

However, the Scottish do not neglect the holiday spirit entirely. The merry-making begins on New Years's Day, called **Hogmanay.** January first is considered Scotland's great national holiday. Immediately after midnight church services, people begin calling and wishing each other a Happy New Year.

A charming custom still remains concerning the first person to step across one's doorsill on New Year's Day. That person is called a "first foot" and is thought to bring either good or bad luck for the coming year (a dark-haired man brings the best luck). Custom dictates that the "first foot" bring a gift or holiday delicacy. In return, the host should offer him a small treat or a drink to be downed in one swallow. The rest of the day is spent visiting family and friends, exchanging greetings and good wishes.

In many villages, groups of boys wearing masks travel from house to house, enacting a folk play. In return for their performance, they are given small gifts of money.

The Serbian Christmas celebration begins on Christmas Eve, when the traditional Yule log or **badnjak** is brought to the family hearth. The log is cut into pieces by the male head of the house and an older son, and members of the family place the pieces on the fire. Wheat is thrown onto the burning **badnjak,** symbolizing the hope for continued good health and prosperity, and straw is strewn throughout the home by the mother and children, representing the unity of the family.

The Christmas Eve fast-supper, **posna vecera,** is strictly composed of traditional foods, such as cooked vegetables, nuts and dried fruits.

A roast suckling pig and other festive dishes are saved for Christmas Day dinner, which begins when the Christmas cake, or **chesnica,** is brought to the table. The **chesnica** may be prepared as a nut pastry or as a simple bread. Either way, a silver coin is placed inside the dough before baking, and the person who receives the piece of pastry containing the coin is supposed to have good luck in the coming year. After the **chesnica** is served, the feasting begins, and celebrating continues for three days.

Serbia

"Hristos Se Rodi"

Slovenia

"Vesele Bozicne"

The Christmas season in this Yugoslavian state begins with St. Nicholas Day on December sixth. It is primarily a children's holiday. Good children look forward to receiving gifts, and naughty children will be reprimanded by the "devils" who accompany the good Saint. St. Nicholas is so revered by the Slovenians that their capital city has a cathedral named in his honor.

One of the unusual holiday customs is the preparation of a special bread called **poprtnjak,** which literally means "bread that is covered with cloth." The bread is placed on the dining room table where it remains covered until Three Kings' Day, when it is distributed to the children.

The corner of the house where the creche is placed is called "God's corner." The father has the sole privilege of setting up the crib. On Christmas Eve, the family gathers around the crib to pray and bless each room of the house with holy water. The barns, sheds and stables are also blessed.

Attending midnight mass is strictly observed. People congregate and proceed to the church carrying lighted torches.

The Festival of the Three Kings (or Epiphany) climaxes the holiday season. On this day youngsters, carrying lighted stars, sing carols from house to house.

Slovenian youngsters in national dress with traditionally decorated Slovenian Christmas tree in background

Spain

"Feliz Navidad"

It is rare to find a home in Spain that does not display a creche at Christmastime. The carved manger scene will usually be placed on a table or mantel and include all the traditional figures as well as the uniquely popular Spanish bull.

Preceding midnight mass on Christmas Eve, the little children dress in peasant costumes and dance around the village Nativity scene to the musical accompaniment of tambourines.

A special meal eaten after midnight mass is called **cena de Nochebuena** or "good night supper." The menu usually includes almond and milk soup, roast lamb, pork or fowl, baked stuffed red cabbage, baked pumpkin, and sweet potato. Almonds, marzipan, and **turron,** a candy loaf of roasted almonds in caramel syrup, are also standard Christmas treats.

Following the feast, the family gathers around the Christmas tree to sing Christmas carols and religious hymns. The tree is sometimes decorated with miniature tambourines, guitars, and paper cribs. Glittering beaded spangles and red paper roses are also popular ornaments.

The children receive their gifts on January sixth, Three Kings' Day, when the Wise Men make their yearly journey to Spain as they once visited Bethlehem so long ago. Children place their shoes outdoors, so the Wise Men can fill them with candy, toys and fruit. Hay is sometimes also left for the weary camels.

The cultures of many nations have merged in this tiny country, and the international flavor of its languages is duplicated in its Christmas traditions. In most parts of Switzerland, the tradition of St. Nicholas is observed, and, as elsewhere, he distributes candy, fruit and toys. Sometimes a parade is held in his honor, with a giant figure of St. Nicholas leading a group of youngsters dressed in long white robes and wearing masks.

In regions observing a variation of this custom, it is **Samichlaus** who is eagerly awaited by youngsters. In other villages, it is "Father Christmas" and his wife, Lucy, who bring gifts to the children.

In rural areas, many folk traditions associated with the Christmas season are popular. For example, the grandmothers select a perfect onion on the night before Christmas and, cutting it in half, peel off twelve layers—one for each month of the coming year. These peelings are then filled with salt. The next morning a weather forecast for each of the twelve months ahead can be made by observing the condition of the salt. The layers in which the salt is dry indicate fair months, while those with damp salt indicate rain. Anyone, of course, with a grandmother's long experience in the kitchen knows what kind of an onion to select and which of the layers would have the most moisture, but it is fun for the children to wonder how grandmother does it.

Marzipan and **Tirggel** cookies shaped in many forms also add to the merriment.

Switzerland

"Froehliche Weinachten"

"Joyeux Noel"

"Buon Natale"

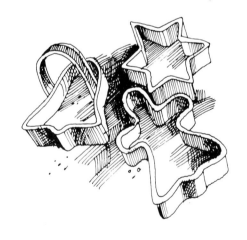

Samichlaus visits the Swiss children.

Ukraine

"Veselykh Svyat"

Christmas traditions in the Ukraine, in the days when that holiday was more generally observed, were largely patterned after those of Lithuania and Poland.

As preparation for Christmas, the house received a thorough cleaning inside and often a fresh coat of whitewash on the outside.

On the farms, a great sheaf of wheat was saved from the summer harvest and placed under an icon in a corner of a room on Christmas Eve. It was usually decorated with ribbons, flowers, and a small wreath of basil.

A twelve course dinner commemorating the twelve apostles was served on Christmas Eve. A porridge with honey called **Koutia** was served to commemorate the Holy Crib. The porridge represented the straw in the manger and the honey, usually accompanied by fruit, symbolized the Infant. After dinner, carolers visited homes to sing traditional Christmas songs.

An old superstition considered it lucky to find a spider web in the house on Christmas. An old Ukrainian legend says that once a poor woman, who was unable to provide any trimmings for her children's Christmas tree, was surprised to find on Christmas morning that spiders had covered the tree with their webs during the night. When the first light of Christmas morning sun struck the tree, the webs turned to silver. Today, one of the unusual ornaments of the Ukrainian tree is a spider and web, believed to ensure good fortune.

Ukrainian girls and Christmas tree, featuring traditional spider ornaments

United States

"Merry Christmas"

Christmas in the United States is the most exciting holiday of the year. The sparkling lights, festive decorations, holiday shopping, and baking all add to the general anticipation and merriment.

The tradition of the Christmas tree, which came to America from Germany, is practiced in many homes. At first, American tree decorations were simple home-made ornaments fashioned from apples, nuts, popcorn, cranberries, and paper. Eventually, glass ornaments, imported from Germany, were used, but today the American-made varieties are popular. A major American contribution to the Christmas tree is the invention of colored electric lights, replacing the use of lighted candles.

Although many Christmas traditions in the United States have been adopted from other countries, the idea of Santa Claus is distinctively American. The name is derived from **Sinter Klass,** which was the pronunciation given to Saint Nicholas by the early Dutch settlers living in New York. A poem written by Clement C. Moore in 1822 helped change the image of the kindly bishop into that of a jolly little old man dressed in a fur-trimmed suit. Children anticipate a visit from Santa Claus on Christmas Eve, when he comes down the chimney and places toys and gifts underneath the Christmas tree.

Many Americans attend church services on Christmas Eve or Christmas morning. There are parties and family gatherings in most homes. An elaborate dinner featuring turkey, ham or roast beef is enjoyed on Christmas Day.

"Merry Christmas," 1879 lithograph by Thomas Nast

Index

Armenia 4

Austria 7

China 8

Croatia 11

Czechoslovakia 12

Egypt 15

England 16

Finland 19

France 20

Germany 23

Greece 24

Hawaii 26

Holland 27

Hungary 28

Iceland 31

Ireland 32

Italy 33

Japan 34

Korea 37

Liberia 38

Lithuania 39

Mexico 40

Philippines 43

Poland 44

Puerto Rico 47

Romania 48

Scandinavia 51

Scotland 52

Serbia 53

Slovenia 55

Spain 56

Switzerland 58

Ukraine 60

United States 63

Publisher, James Kuse
Managing Editor, Ralph Luedtke
Production Editor/Manager, Mark Brunner
Photographic Editor, Gerald Koser
Copy Editor, Barbara Nevid
Designed by, Michele Arrieh